HARCOURT SCIENCE

WORKBOOK

TEACHER'S EDITION

Harcourt School Publishers

Orlando • Boston • Dallas • Chicago • San Diego

www.harcourtschool.com

500
H26
workbook
teachers
ed
gr.1

ISBN 0-15-323717-1

2 3 4 5 6 7 8 9 10 022 2004 2003 2002

Contents

Harcourt

Harcourt

Science Safety

Think ahead.

Be neat and clean.

Be careful.

Do not eat or drink things.

Safety Symbols

Be careful!

Sharp!

Be careful!

Wear an apron.

Wear goggles.

Harcourt

Science Safety

____ I will think ahead.

____ I will read the directions and follow them.

____ I will be neat with my materials.

____ I will take care of all science supplies.

____ I will clean up when I am done.

____ I will return all unused materials to my teacher.

____ I will be careful. I will follow all of the cautions.

____ I will not taste things I am using in an investigation unless my teacher tells me to.

Harcourt

Name _____

LESSON 2
What Are Living and Nonliving Things?

1. Living things need food, water, and air.

2. Animals, plants, and people are living.

3. Nonliving things do not need food, water, or air.

4. Nonliving things do not grow.

LESSON 1
How Do My Senses Help Me Learn?

My 5 senses are

1. sight
2. touch
3. hearing
4. smell
5. taste

Harcourt

Name _____

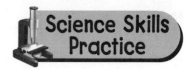

Observe

Draw a line to the sense each person is using.

1. touch •

2. taste •

3. hear •

4. see •

5. smell •

6. Circle all the senses the boy can use to find out about the banana.

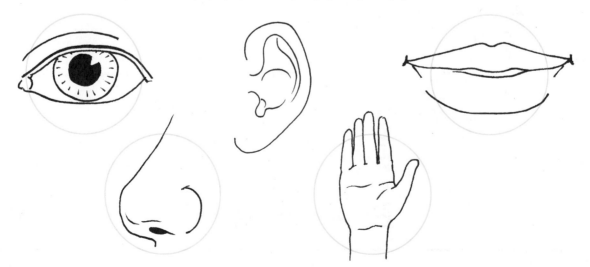

Harcourt

How Do My Senses Help Me Learn?

Match the body part to the sense.

1. sight •

2. hearing •

3. smell •

4. touch •

5. taste •

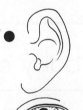

6. Circle all the senses the boy is using.

Harcourt

Name _____

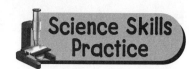

Compare

1. Tell how the baby and the doll are the same.

Both have the same body parts.

_____

_____

_____

2. Tell how the baby and the doll are different.

_____

The baby is a living thing.

_____

The doll is nonliving.

Harcourt

Name _____

What Are Living and Nonliving Things?

Color the living things **red**.
Color the nonliving things **blue**.

chicks, cow, grass, flowers, cat
barn, fence, trough, ground, clouds

1. Flowers grow. Tell one other thing in the picture that will grow.

Answers may include cat, grass, cow, and chicks.

Children may draw their answers in this space.

2. Tell one thing in the picture that is nonliving.

Answers may include fence, barn, and water trough.

Children may draw their answers in this space.

Harcourt

Use with page A15.

Workbook • WB5

Name _____

Living and Nonliving Things

Write the word from the box that best completes each sentence.

living	nonliving	senses

1. You can use your five _____ *senses* to help you learn.

2. Plants, animals, and people are _____ *living* things.

3. Things that do not need food, water, and air are _____ *nonliving* things.

4. Circle the word that tells about the picture.

   living   (nonliving)

Harcourt

Name _____

Sentences

Read the sentences. Draw a line under the first word of each sentence. Then draw a circle around the period in each sentence.

Senses

Your eyes can see a sunset.

Your skin can feel a furry kitten.

Your ears can hear a tapping drum.

Your nose can smell a rose.

Your mouth can taste a sour lemon.

Look at the picture. Write a sentence about the picture. Draw a line under the first word of your sentence. Then draw a circle around the period in your sentence.

_____

- -

_____

Harcourt

Name _____

Write to Describe

A. Choose one of your senses. Draw one living thing and one nonliving thing you learn about with that sense.

Sense _____

Living Thing	Nonliving Thing

B. Write about what you drew.

_____

_____

_____

_____

Harcourt

Unit A, Chapter 2 All About Plants

LESSON 1	LESSON 2	LESSON 3
What Are the Parts of a Plant?	**How Do Plants Grow?**	**What Do Plants Need?**
The parts of a plant are	1. Most plants grow from seeds .	Plants need
1. roots	2. Plants need water .	1. air
2. stem	3. Roots grow in the soil .	2. light
3. leaves		3. water
4. flowers		4. soil

Harcourt

Name _____

Compare

maple tree

daisy

tomato

1. Tell how the plants are the same.

Answers may include: All have leaves

and stems.

2. Tell how the plants are different.

Answers may include: Tree has hard stem,

others have soft stem; daisy has a flower;

tomato has fruit.

Use with page A22.

Harcourt

Name _____

What Are the Parts of a Plant?

1. Label each plant part. Use the words in the box.

roots	stem	leaves	flower

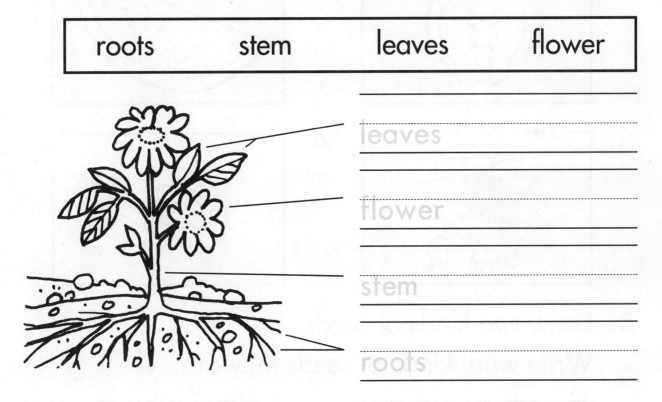

leaves

flower

stem

roots

2. Color the plant part that makes food **green**.

3. Color the plant part that holds the plant in soil and takes in water **yellow**.

4. Color the plant part that moves water from the roots to the leaves **brown**.

5. Color the plant part that makes seeds **red**.

Harcourt

Name _____

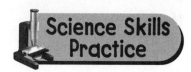

Observe

Circle the seeds in each picture.

1.

2.

3.

4.

5. Draw two kinds of seeds.
Write what kinds of seeds they are.

_____

- - - - - - - - - - - - - - - - -

_____

Harcourt

Name _____

How Do Plants Grow?

1. This is a flower seed. What might the plant look like when it grows?

ρ

Children should draw a plant with flowers.

2. This is a pumpkin seed. What might the plant look like when it grows?

Children should draw a vine with pumpkins on it.

3. Color all the things that grew from seeds.

Harcourt

Name _____

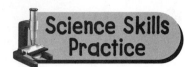

Communicate

1. Draw and color a plant. Show a partner the different parts of your plant.

> Children should draw a plant with roots, stems, leaves, and possibly flowers.

Tell two things that all plants need. Add these things to your drawings.

2. water or soil _____   **3.** light or air _____

Harcourt

Use with page A32.

Name _____

What Do Plants Need?

1. Plants need air to grow. Circle two other
things that plants need to grow.

2. The plant near the
window is growing
well. The plant in
the corner is **not**
growing well.
Tell why.

_____

The plant in the corner is not getting

_____

enough light.

Harcourt

Name _____

Vocabulary Review

All About Plants

Write your answers. Use the words in the box.

flower	leaves	roots
stem	seed	seed coat

1. I hold plants in the soil. What am I?

roots

2. I help hold up the plant. What am I?

stem

3. I make food. What am I?

leaves

4. I make seeds. What am I?

flower

5. Most plants grow from this.

seed

Harcourt

Use with pages A22–A35.

Name _____

Headings

Read the sentences. Circle the heading that would be used with the sentences.

1. Parts of a Plant
Parts of a Carrot
How Plant Parts Help a Plant

Plants have different parts.
Most plants have roots, a stem, and leaves.
Some plants have flowers.

2. Write a heading to go with the sentences and picture.

_____

Accept reasonable answers.

_____

There are different kinds of leaves.
One of the leaves is an oak leaf.
One of the leaves is a maple leaf.

Harcourt

Write to Inform

A. On the plate, draw seeds or a food made with seeds that you like to eat.

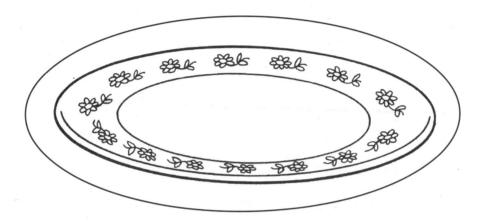

B. Write about the seeds you drew. Tell what kind of plant they would grow to be.

_____

_____

_____

_____

_____

_____

_____

_____

Harcourt

Unit A, Chapter 3 All About Animals

LESSON 1 Animal Needs

Animals need

1. food

2. water

3. air

4. shelter

LESSON 2 Kinds of Animals

5 kinds of animals

1. mammals

2. birds

3. reptiles

4. amphibians

5. fish

LESSON 3 Insects

1. Insects have 6 legs and 3 body parts.

2. Insects lay eggs.

3. Insects have strong body coverings.

LESSON 4 Animal Growth

1. Animals grow to look like their parents.

2. Some animals hatch from eggs.

LESSON 5 Butterfly Growth

1. A butterfly passes through 4 stages.

2. Wings keep butterflies safe.

LESSON 6 Frog Growth

1. A frog is an amphibian.

2. A frog passes through 5 stages.

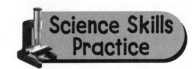

Observe

Each animal is meeting a need. Tell which need. Use words from the box.

shelter	air	water	food

Air is also an acceptable response to items 1, 2, and 3.

1. _____
    shelter
    _____

2. _____
    water
    _____

3. _____
    food
    _____

4. Draw an animal. Show it meeting its needs.

Harcourt

Name _____

What Do Animals Need?

1. Animals need air. Color three other
things this bird needs to live. Children should color
food, water, and nest or tree itself for shelter.

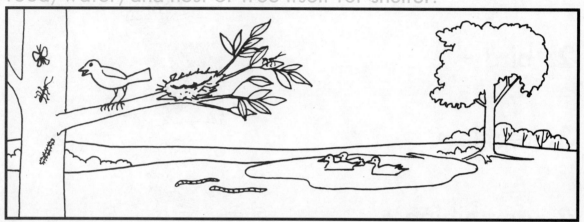

Some animals have sharp teeth. Some have
flat teeth. Match each animal to its teeth.

2.

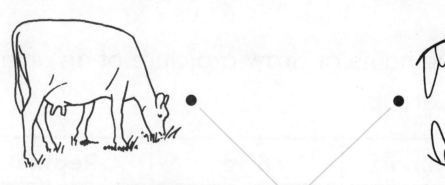

3.

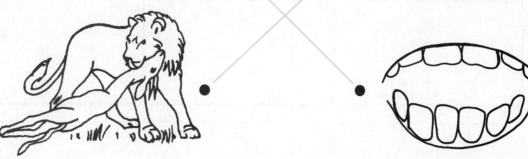

Harcourt

Name _____

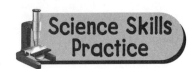

Classify

Match each animal to its body covering.

1. mammal •

2. bird •

3. reptile •

4. amphibian •

5. fish •

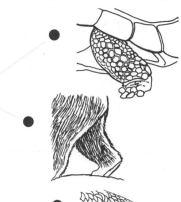

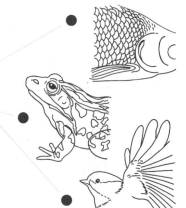

6. Write the name or draw a picture of an animal in each group.

Mammal	Bird	Reptile

_____   _____   _____

_____   _____   _____

Harcourt

What Are Some Kinds of Animals?

Many kinds of animals live in this forest.

1. Color all the amphibians **orange**. frogs

2. Color all the mammals **brown**. deer, raccoon, squirrels

3. Color all the reptiles **green**. turtle, snake

4. Color all the birds **blue**. duck, flying bird, woodpecker

5. Another kind of animal is also in the picture.
Write its name.

_____

fish

 Harcourt

Name _____

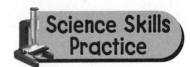
Make a Model

1. Draw the parts so they make an insect.

2. Name this insect.

ant

Harcourt

What Are Insects?

1. Color the animals that are insects.

2. How many body parts does an insect have?

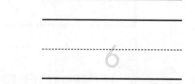

3

3. How many legs does an insect have?

6

4. Draw two kinds of insects. Draw one with wings.

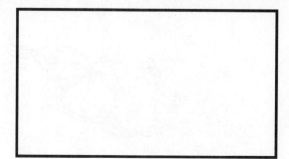

NMU LIBRARY

Harcourt

Name _____

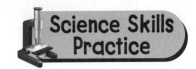

Compare

1. Compare the animals.

	Ways they are the same.	**Ways they are different.**
swan	They are both swans (or birds). They both have feathers.	One is an adult, the other is its young; one is smaller than the other.
dog	They are both dogs. They both have fur.	One is an adult. The other is a puppy.

2. Circle the part that shows how these animals are helping their young.

Harcourt

Use with page A58.

Name _____

How Do Animals Grow?

Match the animal to where it came from.

1.

2.

3.

4.

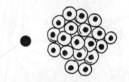

5. What are two things an animal can teach its young?

_____

find food, get shelter, stay warm

_____

_____

_____

Harcourt

Use with page A63.

Name _____

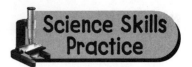

Observe

1. Color the butterflies **red**.
2. Color the larva **blue**.
3. Color the pupa **yellow**.
4. From what does a caterpillar hatch?

   _____

   an egg

   _____

5. What comes out of a pupa?

   _____

   an adult butterfly

   _____

Harcourt

How Does a Butterfly Grow?

Draw a line under the best ending.

1. A caterpillar hatches from an egg. The caterpillar becomes a pupa and makes a hard covering. The pupa changes into a _____.

    larva   <u>butterfly</u>   bigger caterpillar

2. These butterflies live in a field of flowers. They keep safe by hiding. Color the flowers and the butterflies. Help the butterflies hide. Children should color the flowers and the butterflies the same color to help hide the butterflies.

Harcourt

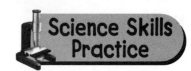

Sequence

1. Tell how the frog grows after it hatches. Write **first**, **next**, or **last** next to each picture.

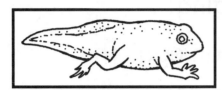

_____
- - - - - - - - - - - - - - - -
next
_____

_____
- - - - - - - - - - - - - - - -
last
_____

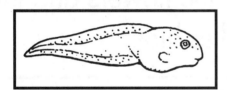

_____
- - - - - - - - - - - - - - - -
first
_____

2. Read the sentences. Number them in sequence. The first one is done for you.

__4__ Young frogs climb onto land.

__3__ Tadpoles use their tails to swim.

1 Frogs lay eggs in the water.

__2__ Tadpoles hatch from the eggs.

Harcourt

Use with page A70.

Name _____

How Does a Frog Grow?

1. Finish each drawing.

tadpole

Children should add a tail.

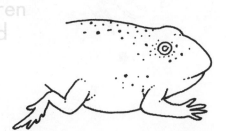

frog

Children should add hind legs and no tail.

2. What part of the tadpole helps it to swim? Color that part **red**. Children should color the tail.

3. Draw where a frog will lay its eggs. Children should draw eggs in the water.

Harcourt

Name _____

All About Animals

1. What kind of animal is it? Draw a line to match.

• • • •

• • • •

amphibian   insect   reptile   mammal

Finish the sentences. Use the words in the box.

hatch	larva	pupa

2. When chicks break out of eggs, they _____ hatch _____.

3. A tiny caterpillar is called a _____ larva _____.

4. A caterpillar makes a hard covering called a _____ pupa _____.

Harcourt

Name _____

Recall Supporting Facts and Details

Read and answer the questions.

Animals and Food

Animals use their body parts to help them get the food they need. A wolf uses its sharp teeth to tear and chew meat. Cows eat grass. They use their flat teeth for chewing. Some birds use their beaks to catch fish. An eagle uses its claws to catch its food.

 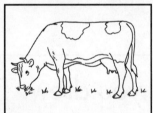  

1. What kind of teeth is used to chew grass?

_____
flat teeth
_____

2. How can an eagle catch its food?

_____
It uses its claws.
_____

3. How can a bird catch a fish?

_____
It uses its beak.
_____

Harcourt

Use with page A44.

Workbook • WB33

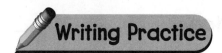
Writing Practice

Write to Inform

A. Draw one of your favorite animals in its home.

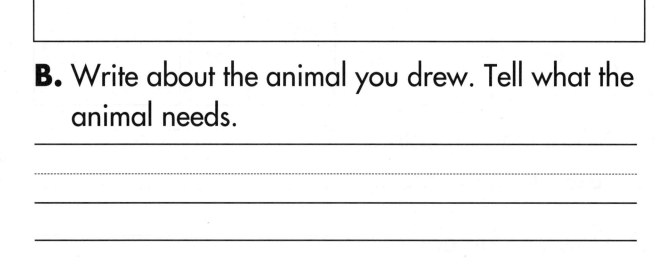

B. Write about the animal you drew. Tell what the animal needs.

_____

- -

_____

_____

- -

_____

- -

_____

Harcourt

Unit B, Chapter 1 Plants and Animals Need One Another

LESSON 1	LESSON 2	LESSON 3
How Do Animals Need Plants?	**How Do Animals Help Plants?**	**How Do We Need Plants and Animals?**
Animals need plants for:	1. Animals move _seeds_ to new places.	1. People need plants and animals for _food_, shelter, and _clothing_.
1. _food_	2. A butterfly may carry _pollen_ from flower to flower.	2. People use plants to make _products_.
2. _shelter_	3. Worms _enrich_ the soil.	
3. _nesting_ materials.		

Harcourt

Name _____

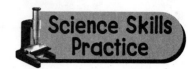

Observe

Animals use plants for different things.

1. Color the plants used for food **green**.

2. One animal uses a plant to make a nest.
Color the nest **yellow**.

3. Color the plants used for shelter **brown**.

4. One animal uses plants to hide.
Tell about that animal.

The butterfly uses plants to hide.

Its color helps it hide in plants.

Harcourt

Name _____

How Do Animals Need Plants?

1. Match each animal to how it is using plants.

• shelter

• food

2. Finish the drawing. Show how an animal uses a log for shelter and food. Children should draw pillbugs or other animals.

Harcourt

Name _____

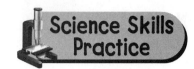

Investigate

A plant grew in Jason's yard. A plant just like it grew in Sara's yard. Sara and Jason investigate how a seed was carried to Sara's yard.

1. Circle what you think moved the seed from one yard to the other.

Children may circle the cat or the dog.

2. Tell how the seed may have moved.

_____

A seed stuck to the dog's or cat's fur. The

_____

dog went from Jason's yard to Sara's yard.

_____

The seed dropped in Sara's yard.

_____

Harcourt

How Do Animals Help Plants?

1. Circle the animals that are helping plants.

2. Tell how a butterfly helps a flower.
Write or draw.

_____

A butterfly carries

_____

pollen from one flower

_____

to another.

_____

_____

Harcourt

Name _____

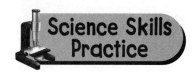

Classify

Circle the things made from plants. Mark
an **X** on the things made from animals.

1.

2.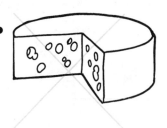

3.

4.

5.

6.

7.

8.

9.

Harcourt

Name _____

How Do We Need Plants and Animals?

Match each product to the animal or plant it came from.

1.  • 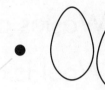 •

2.  •  •

3.  • •

4. • •

5. Tell how an animal can be a helper to a person. Write or draw.

_____

Accept reasonable

_____

answers.

Harcourt

Plants and Animals Need One Another

Draw a line under each sentence that is true.

1. Animals use shelter for food.

2. Wastes can help enrich soil.

3. Wool is an animal product used for clothing.

4. Powder from flowers is called pollen.

Match each word to the correct picture.

5. shelter •

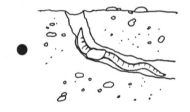

6. enrich •

7. product •

8. pollen •

Harcourt

Use with pages B4–B19.

Name _____

Use Context

Underline the word or words that help you know what the shaded word means.

1. The waste of a worm enriches the soil and makes the soil better for plants.

2. A cat can carry a seed and move it to a new place to grow.

Look at the pictures. Mark an **X** on the animals or insects that carry pollen from flower to flower.

Tell how an animal can carry seeds to a new place.

Answers will vary. Possible response: A cat

can carry seeds to a new place when the

seeds stick to its fur.

Harcourt

Name _____

Write to Persuade

A. Plan an ad for a product made from plants. Draw the product. Make up a name for your product.

Product Name _____

B. Write a sentence telling why people should use your product.

_____

Harcourt

Unit B, Chapter 2 A Place to Live

LESSON 1
What Lives in a Forest?

1. A forest is shady .

2. Plants get the sun they need in the forest.

3. Animals find food and shelter in the forest.

LESSON 2
What Lives in the Desert?

1. A desert is a dry place. There is little rain .

2. Desert plants hold water .

3. Desert animals have ways to stay cool .

LESSON 3
What Lives in a Rain Forest?

1. A rain forest gets a lot of rain .

2. Plants and animals use different levels among the trees for food and shelter .

LESSON 4
What Lives in the Ocean?

1. An ocean is salt water.

2. Ocean animals use plants for food and shelter .

Harcourt

Name _____

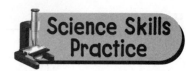

Compare

1. Tell how these leaves are the same.

They both have jagged
edges.

oak

2. Tell how they are different.

They come from different
trees; the oak leaf is more
jagged than the maple.

maple

---

3. Tell how these leaves are the same.

They both have a stem.

rose

4. Tell how they are different.

The rose leaf has many
sharp points, the ivy few
sharp points.

ivy

Harcourt

Use with page B26.

Name _____

What Lives in a Forest?

Answer **yes** or **no**.

1. Are there many trees
in a forest?   _____

2. Does the soil stay dry?   _____

3. Is there a lot of sunlight
on the forest floor?   _____

4. Do some trees grow
tall in a forest?   _____

5. Finish the picture of the forest. Show plants
and animals that live in a forest.

Harcourt

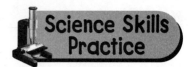

Draw a Conclusion

These animals live in a desert. Put an **X**
where an animal might go to stay cool
in the daytime. Color the picture.

Children may put an X on the burrow near the cactus or in the shade of the rock or prickley pear cactus. Accept either answer.

Harcourt

What Lives in the Desert?

1. Mark an **X** on the plants and animals that do not belong in the desert.

Note: Frogs may appear in a desert during the rainy season.

2. Circle the words that tell about a desert.

dry	wet	rainy
sunny	cactus	oak tree

Name _____

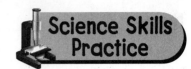

Communicate

1. Tell about plants that grow where there is little light. Write or draw.

_____
- -
_____

_____
- -
_____

_____
- -
_____

Children should show or tell about long, leggy plants that are light in color.

2. Tell about plants that grow where there is a lot of light. Write or draw.

_____
- -
_____

_____
- -
_____

_____
- -
_____

Children should show or tell about healthy, green plants.

Harcourt

Concept Review

What Lives in a Rain Forest?

1. Draw animals that live at each level of the rain forest.

Accept any reasonable response. Possible answers: scarlet macaw near treetops, sloths in middle, iguana and matamata turtle in low level.

Draw a line under the best answer.

2. Most rain forests are _____.

cool and dry   wet and warm   wet and cool

3. Plants that need a lot of light live at the _____ of the rain forest.

bottom   middle   top

Name _____

Classify

Color the animals that live in the ocean.
Mark **X** through the animals that do **not**
live in the ocean.

1.
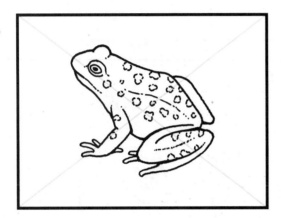

2.
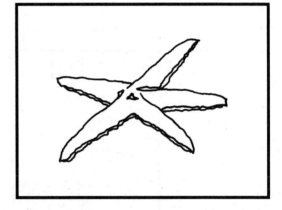

3.

4.

5.
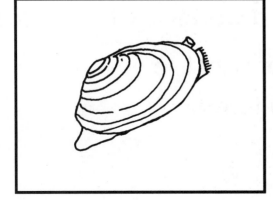

6.
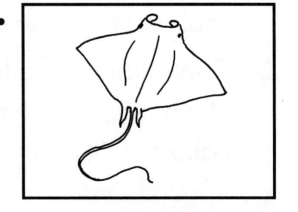

Harcourt

Name _____

What Lives in the Ocean?

1. Complete the picture. Show what helps the animal swim fast to catch food.

Children should add fins and a tail.

2. Circle the body parts that help the animals swim and steer.

3. Add algae to the picture. Draw the algae where it lives. Children should show algae near the water's surface.

Harcourt

Name _____

A Place to Live

Label each picture. Use the words in the box.

| algae | desert | forest | ocean | rain forest |

1. _____
   desert

2. _____
   ocean

3. _____
   algae

4. _____
   rain forest

5. _____
   forest

Harcourt

Use with pages B26–B41.

Name _____

Relate Pictures to Text

Rain forests are wet and warm. Plants and animals live at different levels of the rain forest. The rain forest gives plants and animals what they need to live.

1. What clues does the picture give to help you decide how the leopard is meeting its needs?

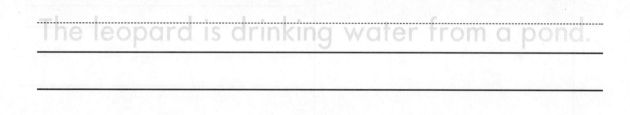

The leopard is drinking water from a pond.

_____

_____

_____

2. What clues does the picture give to help you decide how the orchid is meeting its needs?

_____

Sunlight is reaching the top of the rain forest.

_____

_____

Harcourt

Name _____

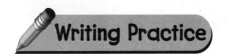

Write to Describe

A. Draw a plant or an animal that lives at each level of the rain forest. Accept all reasonable answers.

In the treetops

_____
- - - - - - - - - - - - - - - - - - -
_____
- - - - - - - - - - - - - - - - - - -
_____

In the middle of the branches

_____
- - - - - - - - - - - - - - - - - - -
_____
- - - - - - - - - - - - - - - - - - -
_____

On the ground

_____
- - - - - - - - - - - - - - - - - - -
_____
- - - - - - - - - - - - - - - - - - -
_____

B. Write describing words next to each picture you drew.

Harcourt

Unit C, Chapter 1 Earth's Land

LESSON 1 What Can We Observe About Rocks?	LESSON 2 What Are Fossils?	LESSON 3 What Have We Learned from Fossils?
1. There are many different kinds of rocks.	1. Plants and animals lived on Earth long ago.	1. An extinct plant or animal is no longer living.
2. People use rocks in different ways.	2. Fossils are the parts of plants or animals that lived long ago.	2. Plants and animals today have changed from long ago.

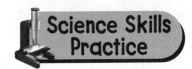

Classify

1. Classify the rocks. Color the large rocks **yellow**. Color the small rocks **blue**.

2. Classify the rocks another way. Color the smooth rocks **red**. Color the rough rocks **green**.

Harcourt

Use with page C4.

Name _____

What Can We Observe About Rocks?

1. Color the rocks **red**. Color the sand **yellow**.

2. People use rocks in different ways. Draw a picture that shows one way people use rocks.

Children should show a building, rock, gravel road, or other use of rocks. Some may show glass objects.

Harcourt

Name _____

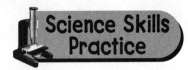

Make a Model

1. This leaf could become a fossil. Draw what the fossil might look like.

Student drawings should show leaf imprint on rock.

2. Make a drawing of some other thing that could become a fossil.

Student drawings will vary but may show a shell, starfish, or animal footprint.

Harcourt

What Are Some Kinds of Fossils?

Draw a line from the fossil to the living thing that made the fossil.

1.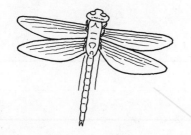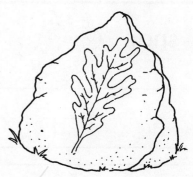

2.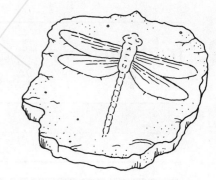

3.

Harcourt

Name _____

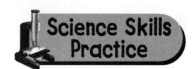

Compare

Describe each kind of fossil. Use the words in the box.

extinct animal	sea animal	plant

1. snail

_____

sea animal

_____

- -

_____

2. trilobite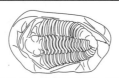

_____

extinct animal

_____

- -

_____

3. fern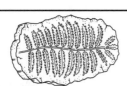

_____

plant

_____

- -

_____

Harcourt

Use with page C12.

Name _____

How Do Different Fossils Compare?

1. Color the plant fossils green. Color the animal fossils red. green: 2 leaf fossils; red: 2 footprints

2. Circle the fossil of the animal that is extinct.

3. Mark an X over the fossil that shows the largest animal.

Harcourt

Name _____

Earth's Land

Write a word to fill in each blank.

rock	fossils	extinct	sand

1. Tiny pieces of rock are called _____. *sand*

2. Kinds of plants or animals that are no longer

   living are _____. *extinct*

3. The parts and imprints of a plant or animal that

   lived long ago are called _____. *fossils*

4. Fossils are usually found in _____. *rock*

Label the picture.

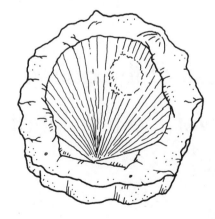

shell fossil

Use with pages C4–C15.

Harcourt

Name _____

Use Graphic Sources for Information

Kinds of Fossils There are many different types of fossils. Some are from animals, and others are from plants. Look at the pictures below. Tell whether each fossil is from a plant or an animal.

_____

plant

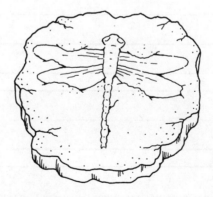

_____

animal

Harcourt

Tell a Story

A. Draw a picture of a starfish in rock.

B. Write a story about what may have happened to the starfish.

Accept reasonable responses

Harcourt

Unit C, Chapter 2 Our Natural Resources

LESSON 1
What Are Natural Resources?

1. Something found in nature that people use is a natural resource .

2. A mineral is a nonliving thing found in nature.

LESSON 2
Where Is Air on Earth?

1. You can feel air but you can't see, smell, or taste it.

2. Plants and animals need air to live.

LESSON 3
Where Is Fresh Water Found?

1. Fresh water is found in most streams, rivers ,and lakes .

2. People need clean , fresh water.

LESSON 4 How Can People Take Care of Resources?

Three things people can do to take care of resources are:

reduce , reuse , and recycle .

Harcourt

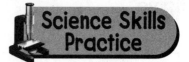

Gather and Record Data

Look at the natural resources found here. How are they used? Record your data in the chart.

Natural Resource	How It Is Used
soil	to grow plants for food
water	for drinking
apple tree	as food for people

Harcourt

Concept Review

What Are Natural Resources?

Match the pictures to tell how people use natural resources.

1.

2.

3.

4. Draw how people use soil to get food. Color the soil brown.

Harcourt

Name _____

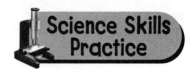

Infer

Air is all around. You can not see air. But you can see what it does.

1. Circle in the picture the things that air is moving.

2. Put an **X** on something filled with air.

3. Color all the living things. They use air, too.

Children should color the girl sitting, the boy standing, fish, trees, grass, flowers.

Harcourt

Name _____

Where Is Air on Earth?

Color where the air is in each picture.

1.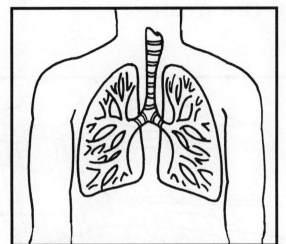
Children should color lungs.

2.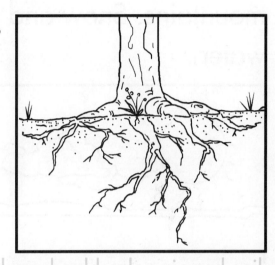
Children should color air and soil.

3.
Children should color air and water.

4.
Children should color air.

Answer **yes** or **no**.

5. You can see air. _____
no

6. You can feel air. _____
yes

Harcourt

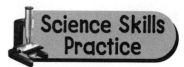

Draw a Conclusion

Rain and melted snow run down mountains. Snow and rain are fresh water.

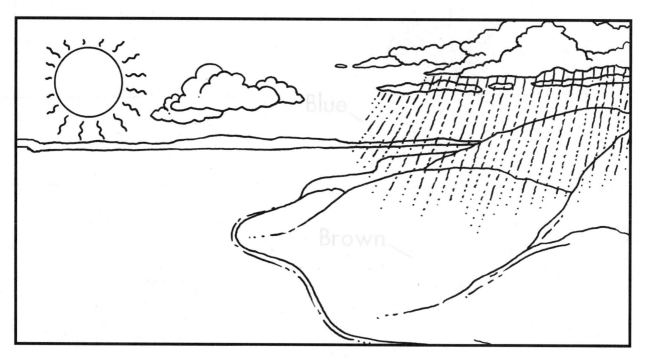

1. Color the fresh water **blue**.
2. Color the mountains **brown**.
3. Tell how you use fresh water.

_____

Answers will vary:
_____
_____

drinking, cooking, and washing.
_____
_____

Harcourt

Use with page C32.

Name _____

Where Is Fresh Water Found?

Match to tell how people use fresh water.

1.

• cooking

2.

• washing

• drinking

3.

4. Draw a freshwater lake. Color it **blue**.

Harcourt

Name _____

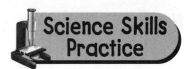

Communicate

1. Write a sentence. Tell how this milk carton is being reused.

_____

The sentence should communicate that the milk

_____

carton is being reused as a pot for plants.

2. Susie is making a drawing with paper and crayons. Write a sentence. Tell how Susie can use less paper.

_____

The sentence should communicate that Susie

_____

can use both sides of the paper.

Harcourt

Name _____

How Can People Take Care of Resources?

1. Water is a natural resource. Which picture shows how to use <u>less</u> water? Mark an **X** over the picture that shows how the girl can use less water.

Circle the best answer.

2. What helps natural resources last longer?

recycling   throwing away

3. What is something you can recycle at home?

newspaper   food

4. What happens if Earth's minerals are used up?

more will grow   there will be no more

Harcourt

Our Natural Resources

1. Color the fresh water blue. Color the air yellow. Circle the river. Air should be colored yellow.

Y

Fill in the blank. Use the words in the box.

reuse	reduce	natural resource	recycle

2. A ___natural resource___ is something found in nature that people can use.

3. When people use less of something, they ___reduce___ their use of them.

4. You can ___reuse___ something by using it again.

5. When you ___recycle___, you collect cans and newspapers to be made into new things.

Harcourt

Name _____

Recall Supporting Facts and Details

Fresh Water Fresh water is found in lakes, rivers, and streams. Rain is fresh water. People use fresh water for drinking, cooking, and washing.

Look at each picture. **X** the pictures that show fresh water.

Harcourt

Name _____

Write a Story

A. Draw a picture of recycling at your school.

[drawing box]

B. Write a story about your picture. Include details about what you observe.

Story should describe what is being recycled and why recycling helps save natural resources.

Harcourt

Use with pages C44–C45.

Unit D, Chapter 1 Measuring Weather

LESSON 1

What Is Weather?

1. Weather is what the air outside is like.

2. Weather changes from day to day, and season to season.

LESSON 2

What Is Temperature?

1. Temperature is how hot or cold it is.

2. Temperature is measured with a thermometer.

LESSON 3

What Is Wind?

1. Wind is moving air.

2. Wind changes direction and speed.

LESSON 4

What Makes Clouds and Rain?

1. Clouds form when warm air meets cooler air.

2. Earth's water moves in a water cycle.

Harcourt

Name _____

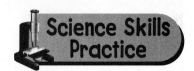

Compare

1. Tell how the pictures are the same and different.
Write your answers in the chart.

My Chart	
Same	**Different**

Possible answers:
• children walking
• buildings
• storekeeper selling fruit
	Possible answers:
	• one rainy, one sunny
	• children are dressed
	  differently & carrying
	  umbrella
	• sky looks different
	• fruit is under canopy
	• children are carrying
	  their books in a bag

2. Color the picture that shows sunny weather.

Children should color the first picture.

Harcourt

Use with page D4.

What Is Weather?

Match each picture to the words that describe the weather.

1.  •   • warm and wet

2.  •   • mostly cloudy

3.  •   • sunny

4.  •   • cold and wet

Answer **yes** or **no**.

5. Is the weather the same every day?   _no_

6. When the air outside changes, does the weather change?   _yes_

Harcourt

Name _____

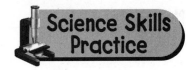

Measure

Temperature is measured in degrees.
Draw a **red** line in each thermometer
to show the temperature.

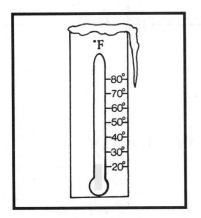 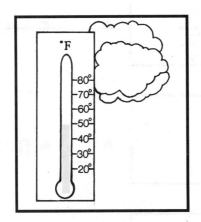 

1. 20 degrees   **2.** 50 degrees   **3.** 80 degrees

4. Make an **X** on the picture that shows the
warmest temperature.

5. Color the jacket you would wear when the
temperature is 20 degrees.

Harcourt

Name _____

What Is Temperature?

Write **high** or **low** to tell about the temperature.

1. _____   **2.** _____   **3.** _____

Tell about each season. Use the words in the box.

hot	warm	cold	cool

4. Fall is often

_____
_____ .

5. Spring is often

_____
_____ .

6. Winter is often

_____
_____ .

7. Summer is often

_____
_____ .

8. Circle the picture that has a cooler temperature.

Harcourt

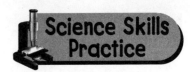

Observe

You can observe the wind. Use arrows.
Show which direction the wind is blowing.

1.

2.

3.
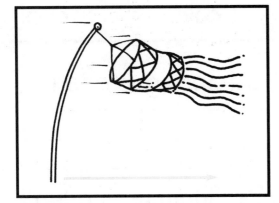

4.

5. Tell how you know which way the wind is blowing.

The wind blows loose objects. The direction

the objects move is the same as the wind

direction.

Harcourt

Name _____

What Is Wind?

1. Circle the picture that shows the wind blowing hard.

2. Tell why you picked that picture.

The wind held up the sail.

3. The wind is keeping up the kite. Draw an **arrow** to show which way the wind is blowing.

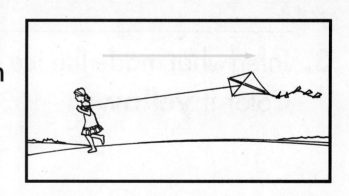

4. The wind is blowing gently. Finish the picture of the flag.

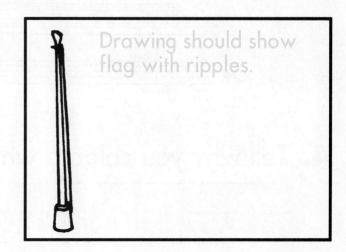

Drawing should show flag with ripples.

Harcourt

Infer

NOTE: Children likely will
have observed this at
home as one way to
indicate whether
something is hot.

1. Infer which cup has hot water in it.
Make an **X** over the picture.

2. Tell why you chose the picture you did.

The cup with steam is hot.

3. Infer what made the ice cream melt.
Color it **yellow**. Children should color the sun.

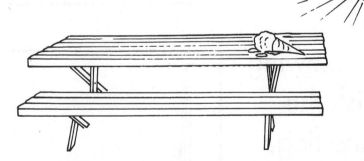

4. Tell why you colored what you did.

The sun is hot. It melts cold things like ice cream.

Harcourt

Name _____

Concept Review

What Makes Clouds and Rain?

1. Finish the water cycle. Draw the missing arrow.

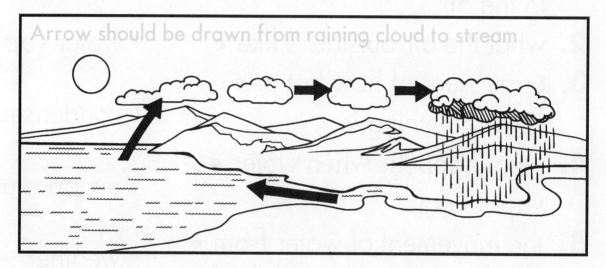

Arrow should be drawn from raining cloud to stream

2. This puddle was left after a hard rain. What happened to it? Circle the best answer.

a. An animal drank the puddle.

b. The water evaporated.

c. The puddle blew away.

Harcourt

Measuring Weather

Match the phrases and the words.

1. water you can not see • in the air

2. what the air outside is like •

3. a measure of how hot or • cold something is

4. what happens when water • vapor cools

5. the movement of water from • the Earth to the air and back

6. what happens when water • changes to water vapor

• temperature

• water vapor

• condenses

• evaporates

• weather

• water cycle

Tell about the picture. Use one of the words. Underline the word.

wind   thermometer

7. _____
   The thermometer shows
   _____
   60 degrees.
   _____

Harcourt

Name _____

Reading Skills Practice

Arrange Events in Sequence

Read the sentences. Then write the sentences in the right order on the lines below.

Clouds and Rain

The water drops may join and get heavier. Then they fall to Earth as rain, hail, sleet, or snow. Tiny drops of water form clouds.

Tiny drops of water form clouds.

The water drops may join and get heavier.

Then they fall to Earth as rain, hail,

sleet, or snow.

This cloud shows water drops falling as rain. Make a drawing of what might happen to the water when it falls to Earth.

Drawings will vary but should depict water making a puddle, falling onto the ground, or filling a water source.

Use with page D18.

Harcourt

Workbook • WB89

Write a Story

A. Plan a story about the water cycle. Draw a picture for each step.

First

Next

Last

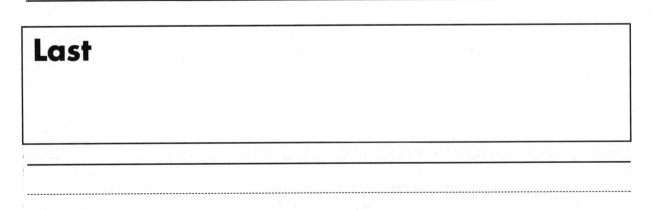

B. Write one sentence to explain each picture.

Harcourt

Unit D, Chapter 2 The Sky and the Seasons

LESSON 1 What Can We See in the Sky?

1. You can see the sun, stars, and moon in the sky.

2. The sun is a star.

LESSON 4 What Is Summer?

1. Summer has the most hours of daylight.

2. The air is warmer in summer than in spring.

LESSON 2 Why Do We Have Day and Night?

1. The sun warms our land, air, and water.

2. When Earth rotates we have day and night.

LESSON 5 What Is Fall?

1. Fall has cooler air than summer.

2. Plants stop growing.

3. Animals have less food.

LESSON 3 What Is Spring?

1. A season is a time of the year.

2. Spring has warmer air than winter.

LESSON 6 What Is Winter?

1. Winter has fewer hours of daylight than fall.

2. Some animals eat stored food.

Communicate

1. Finish the chart. Look at the day sky and the
night sky. Record what you see.

Things in the Day Sky	Things in the Night Sky
cloud	moon
sun	stars
bird	
airplane	

2. Write a sentence that tells about the night sky.

Answers will vary.

Harcourt

Name _____

What Can We See in the Sky?

1. Circle the things that are found in the night sky.

crescent moon and stars should be circled

Circle the words that best finish the sentence.

2. Stars are objects in the sky that _____.

    are very close   (give off light)   you see in daylight

3. Mars, Venus, and Earth are all _____.

    stars   moons   (planets)

Harcourt

Name _____

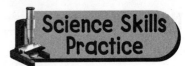

Make a Model

1. Draw an arrow from the sun to Earth.

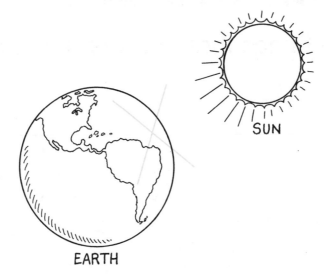

SUN

EARTH

2. Mark an X on the part of Earth the sun shines on.

3. Look at the X. Is it day or night there?

day

4. Draw what the sky looks like during the day.

Accept any reasonable response. Children might draw the sun, clouds, or birds in the sky.

Harcourt

Use with page D30.

Name _____

Why Do We Have Day and Night?

1. Sometimes it is day, and sometimes it is night. Look at the X marked on Earth. Circle the picture that shows it is night where the X is.

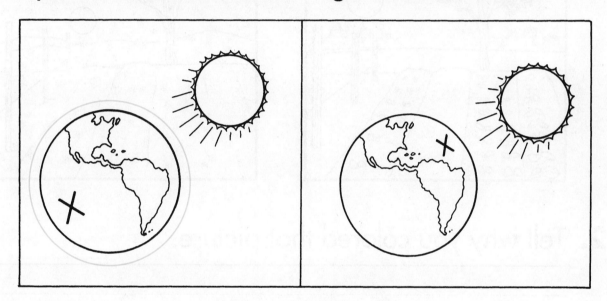

Circle the words that best finish the sentence.

2. The sun gives off _____.

daylight and darkness   stars and moons   heat and light

3. Earth is always moving because it _____.

rotates   moves   shakes

Harcourt

Name _____

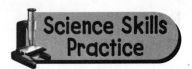

Infer

1. Juan would like to grow beans. Color the picture that shows the best time to plant the seeds. Children color picture on left.

2. Tell why you colored that picture.

_____

Children should indicate that plants sprout

_____

when it is warm outside and spring rains

_____

soak seeds.

_____

3. Circle the words that tell about what a seed needs to begin to grow.

water   warmth   light   air

WB96 • Workbook   **Use with page D34.**

Harcourt

What Is Spring?

1. Circle the things that are found in spring.

2. Circle the words that best finish the sentence.

Spring has _____.

cooler air   falling leaves   (more hours of daylight)

3. Draw how growing plants help young animals.

Drawing should indicate animals using plants as food.

Harcourt

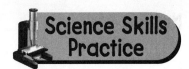

Order

1. Write the temperatures from coolest to hottest.

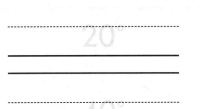

_____

_____
_____

_____
_____

_____
_____

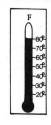 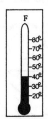

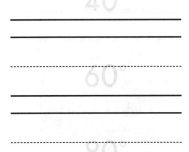

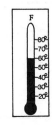 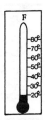

2. These words tell how a plant will grow. Draw pictures to show how a plant will grow.

seed   sprout   flower

Use with page D38.

Harcourt

What Is Summer?

Animals look different in spring and summer.
Tell which season each picture shows.

1. _____ summer _____

2. _____ spring _____

3. _____ spring _____

4. _____ summer _____

5. Draw flowers and trees in summer.

Drawing should show sun and plants with leaves, flowers, and possibly fruit.

Harcourt

Name _____

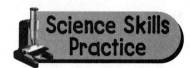

Predict

1. Draw what these trees will look
like when they have fruit ready for
picking. Color the fruit on each tree.

Trees should have appropriate fruit drawn in.

orange tree

cherry tree

2. In spring, this kitten was born. In summer, it
grew. Draw what the kitten will look like next.

Drawing
should indicate
adult cat.

Harcourt

Name _____

What Is Fall?

Circle the answer that fits the sentence best.

1. The season that follows summer is _____ .

spring   (fall)

2. In fall there are _____ hours of daylight.

(less)   more

3. In some places, leaves change in fall. Draw one of those places. Color it.

```
┌─────────────────────────────────────┐
│                                       │
│                                       │
│                                       │
│                                       │
│                                       │
└─────────────────────────────────────┘
```

4. It is fall. Tell what this animal is doing.

_____

The animal is gathering food for the winter.

_____

Harcourt

Name _____

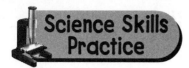

Investigate

1. Circle the gloves that are best for keeping warm.

2. Carol has a pair of boots. One boot has a hole. Tell how Carol could investigate which boot has a hole. Draw pictures of the things she could use to help. This space is for students to draw pictures.

Accept reasonable suggestions. Students may suggest a bowl of water into which Carol could dip her boot. Look for

evidence that students understand that they should find a way of testing each boot for leaks.

Harcourt

Name _____

What Is Winter?

1. Color the winter tree **blue**. Color the
spring tree **green**. Color the summer
tree **yellow**. Color the fall tree **red**.
Label the season for each picture.

green

_____

spring

yellow

_____

summer

red

_____

fall

blue

_____

winter

2. Tell what a plant might look like in winter.

_____

In winter plants look dead.

_____

Harcourt

Name _____

The Sky and the Seasons

Label each picture. Use the words in the box.

| spring | sun | summer | fall | moon | winter |

1. _____ spring

2. _____ winter

3. _____ fall

4. _____ summer

These sentences are **false**. Change the underlined words to make the sentences **true**.

5. We have day and night because Earth <u>stops</u>.

_____ rotates

6. The <u>sun</u> is the brightest object in the sky at night.

_____ moon

Harcourt

Name _____

Identify Cause and Effect

Plants and Animals in Summer Read the sentences. Draw an arrow from the cause to the effect.

Cause	Effect
1. Lots of sunlight helps plants grow.	They begin to look like adult birds.
2. Young birds lose their first feathers.	They become strong and fast.
3. Young foals eat and grow.	Flowers begin to form.

Wearing white can help keep you cool on a hot day. Write how this boy might feel.

_____

- - - - - - - - - - - - - - - - - -

_____

Child should indicate the boy feels hot.

Harcourt

Use with page D36.

Name _____

Write to Describe

Draw your neighborhood as it looks in each season. Write a sentence to describe each picture.

Spring	Summer

_____

- -

_____

- -

_____

Fall	Winter

_____

- -

_____

- -

_____

Harcourt

Use with pages D52–D53.

Name _____

Unit E, Chapter 1 Investigate Matter

LESSON 1 What Can We Observe About Solids?

1. Everything around us is matter .

2. Solids are matter that keep their shape .

3. Solids can be sorted in many ways .

LESSON 2 What Can We Observe About Liquids?

1. Matter that flows is called a liquid .

2. Liquids take the shape of what they are poured into.

3. Some liquids mix with water, but oil does not.

LESSON 3 What Objects Sink or Float?

1. Some objects float and some objects sink .

2. Changing the shape of an object helps it sink or float.

LESSON 4 What Solids Dissolve in Liquids?

1. Some solids dissolve in liquids.

2. Soil and sand do not dissolve in water.

LESSON 5 What Can We Observe About Gases?

1. Gas spreads out and takes the shape of its container.

2. You can not see gases but you can see what they do.

LESSON 6 How Can We Change Objects?

1. You can change objects by rolling or bending them.

2. You can change objects by freezing or mixing them.

Name _____

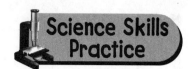

Classify

1. Group the objects that are the same. Draw your groups in the chart.

My Groups	
Group 1	**Group 2**
marbles	present
beach ball	book
grapes	blocks

2. Tell why you grouped the objects as you did.

Most children will group the materials by

shape—those that are round or have corners

Harcourt

Name _____

Concept Review

What Can We Observe About Solids?

1. Draw something that is matter.

Children can draw any object—solid, liquid, or gas.

2. Color the solids **red**.

Everything except
the spilled milk
and air should be
colored.

3. How is this man changing a solid?

He is carving the wood

and changing its shape.

Harcourt

Name _____

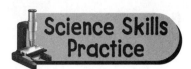

Use Numbers

1. Circle the container you think
has more water.

Accept any response;
most children will indicate Container B.

A　　　**B**

2. Circle the tool you could use to measure
the water.

  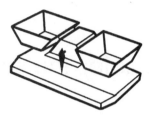

3. Jill measured the water in each container.
Both containers had 12 ounces. Circle the
words that tell about the containers.

Container A _____.

　a. has more water than Container B

　b. has the same amount of water as Container B

　c. has less water than Container B

4. Why does B look as if it has more water than A?

_____

Container B is taller. _____

Harcourt

Name _____

What Can We Observe About Liquids?

1. Draw liquids in the containers.

Children should show liquids taking the shape of each container.

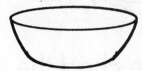 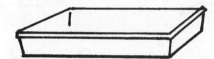 

2. Circle the liquid that does not mix with water.

3. Circle the things that are liquid.

Harcourt

Name _____

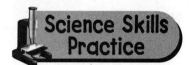
Gather and Record Data

1. Observe the picture. Record in the chart the liquids and solids.

Matter	
Liquids	**Solids**
Children may write or draw fountain spray, fountain water, and spilled soft drink.	Children may write or draw bench, bush, tree, ball, soft drink can, and rocks.

2. How many solids are there? _____ 6

3. How many liquids are there? _____ 3

Harcourt

Name _____

What Objects Sink or Float?

Circle **float** or **sink** for each picture.

1.

float   (sink)

2.

(float)   sink

3.

(float)   sink

4.

float   (sink)

5. Draw something that floats and something that sinks. Color the object that floats **red**. Color the object that sinks **blue**.

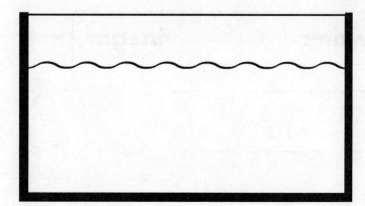

Harcourt

Name _____

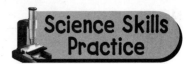
Form a Hypothesis

Use terms from the box to help you form a
hypothesis. Write it.

1. A tea bag is placed in a cup of hot water.

water	dissolve	tea

_____

The tea will dissolve in the water.

2. A rock is dropped into a container
of water.

rock	water	sink

_____

The rock will sink in the water.

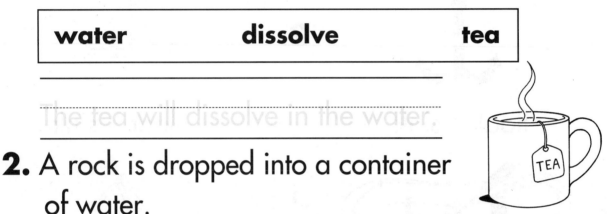

3. A chef stirs a cup filled with vinegar and water.

mix	water	vinegar

_____

The vinegar will mix with water.

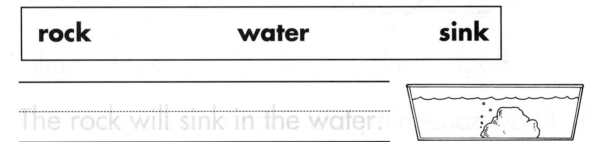

Harcourt

Name _____

What Solids Dissolve in Liquids?

1. Circle the solids that dissolve in water.

2. Circle the solids that do not dissolve in water.

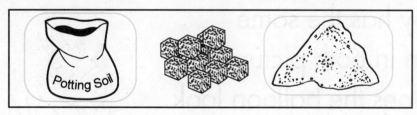

3. In what temperature of a liquid will solids dissolve faster?

hot   cold

4. Complete the sentence below.
   A solid dissolves in a liquid when

_____

the solids mixes completely with the liquid.

_____

Name _____

Draw a Conclusion

1. These spoons had different liquids on them. Why is one liquid still on the spoon?

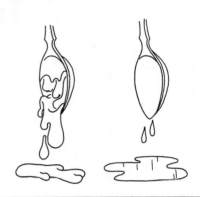

It is thicker and takes more
_____

time to run off the spoon.
_____

2. The boy has the same balloon in both pictures. Why does the balloon look different in the second picture?

It has air in it.
_____

_____

3. What happened to the clay?

It was molded into a ball.
_____

_____

Harcourt

Name _____

What Can We Observe About Gases?

1. There is gas in each container. Color the space the gas takes up.

Children should color the entire space of each container.

2. Color where the gas is in this liquid.

Children should color
the bubbles.

3. You can not see air.
How do you know it is here?

_____

Possible answer: Wind is blowing the balloon.

Harcourt

Use with page E23.   **Workbook • WB117**

Name _____

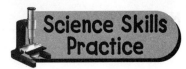

Investigate

1. These pictures are not finished. Finish
each picture a different way.

2. These pictures are the same. Color
each picture to make it look different.

Use with page E24.

Harcourt

Name _____

How Can We Change Objects?

1. This toy is made of wire. Draw how you could bend it to make it look different.

Figure should be changed to look different from the starting picture.

2. You could change this paper with scissors. Draw how it would look after you cut it.

Drawing should be star shaped.

3. Finish the sentence. Circle the best word.

_____ changes liquid juice to a frozen ice pop.

Melting   (Freezing)   Mixing

Harcourt

Use with page E27.   **Workbook • WB119**

Matter

Write your answer. Use the words in the box.

gas	liquid	matter

1. I am all around you. What am I? _____

matter or gas

2. I take up the shape of my container. What am I? _____

gas or liquid

3. I can flow fast or slow. What am I? _____

a liquid

Match the word to the picture that tells about it.

4. solids •

5. sink •

6. float •

7. change •

8. dissolve •

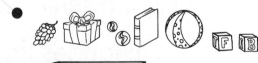
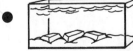

Harcourt

Name _____

Use Graphic Sources for Information

How Objects React on Water

Use the chart to answer the questions.

Objects That Sink	Objects That Float
marble	beach ball
rock	driftwood
anchor	toy boat
	plastic cup

1. How many objects float? _4_ How many sink? _3_

2. Circle the object that you might find at the bottom of a pond.

3. Which objects would be best used in a fish tank? Circle your answers.

Harcourt

Use with page E10.

Name _____

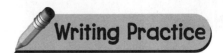

Write to Compare and Contrast

A. Draw a container of a thin liquid and a container of a thick liquid that you like to drink. Label your pictures.

Thin Liquid: _____	**Thick Liquid:** _____

B. Write about how these liquids are alike.

Answers will vary but should describe how the
_____
liquids are alike.
_____

C. Write about how these liquids are different.

Answers will vary but should include that one
_____
liquid is thin and the other liquid is thick.
_____

Harcourt

Use with pages E30–E31.

Unit E, Chapter 2 Making Sound

LESSON 1	LESSON 2	LESSON 3
What Are Sounds?	How Are Sounds Different?	What Sounds Do Instruments Make?
1. Sound is made when objects _vibrate_ ___.	**1.** Sounds are _different_ ___.	**1.** Musical instruments make _sound_ when a part vibrates.
2. You hear _sounds_ all around you.	**2.** Sounds can be quiet or _loud_ ___.	**2.** Each instrument has its own _sound_ ___.
	3. The _pitch_ of a sound is how high or low the sound is.	

Harcourt

Investigate

1. This guitar makes sound. Color the part that vibrates to make sound.

guitar strings should be colored

Match the sound to the thing that makes it.

2. ring

3. boom

4. shhh

Harcourt

Name _____

What Are Sounds?

1. Mark an X on all the things that are making sounds.

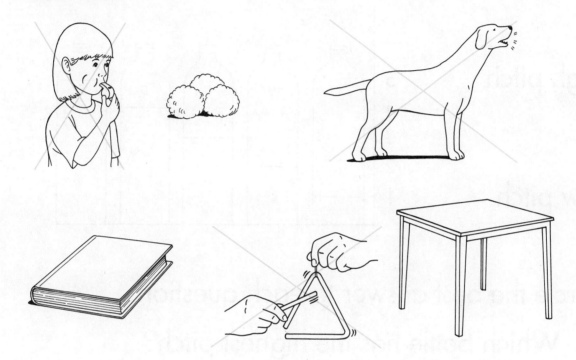

Circle the word that best finishes each sentence.

2. Sound is made when things _____.

       stand still   (vibrate)

3. When strings on a violin _____
stop vibrating, the sound _____.

     (stops)   gets louder

Harcourt

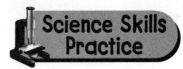

Use Numbers

Each bottle has a different pitch.

high pitch

low pitch

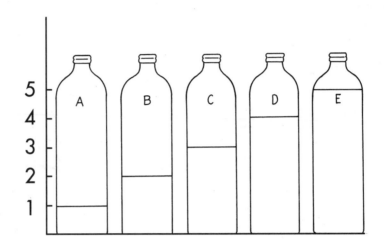

Circle the best answer to each question.

1. Which bottle has the highest pitch?

Bottle A   Bottle C   Bottle E

2. Which bottle has the lowest pitch?

Bottle A   Bottle C   Bottle E

Harcourt

Name _____

How Are Sounds Different?

1. Circle the things that make loud sounds. Mark an **X** over the things that make soft sounds.

2. Write the word that best finishes the sentence.

loud	low

_____

The pitch is how high or ___low___ the sound is.

Harcourt

Name _____

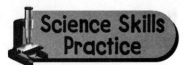

Form a Hypothesis

1. What kinds of sounds do these instruments make? Draw a line to the word in the box that tells your answer.

tap	honk	ding

2. What part of this instrument is missing? Draw what is missing.

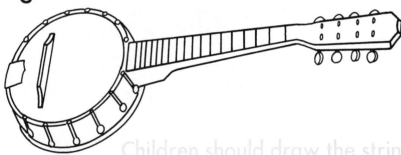

Children should draw the strings.

3. Write a sentence about how you can make the banjo make noise.

_____

The sentences should indicate that plucking

_____

or picking strings makes them vibrate.

_____

Harcourt

Use with page E46.

Name _____

What Sounds Do Instruments Make?

1. Color the part of the instrument that vibrates to make sound. The following should be colored: drum head, triangle, strings on violin.

These children are making music.

Write a sentence that tells how the musical instruments are different.

_____

Sentences should indicate that the instruments sound different from one another and are played differently.

_____

Use with page E49.

Workbook • WB129

Harcourt

Name _____

Making Sound

These sentences are false. Change the underlined word to make the sentence true.

1. To move back and forth very fast is to <u>hum</u>.

_____

vibrate

_____

2. <u>Music</u> is how high or low a sound is. _____

Pitch

Circle the word that best finishes the sentence.

_____

3. Everything you hear is _____ .

loud   (sound)   soft

4. A _____ is something used to make music.

(musical instrument)   loud   pitch

Look at the picture.
X the part that vibrates.

Harcourt

Name _____

Recall Supporting Facts and Details

Read the story below. Then answer the questions.

Max likes to make his guitar sound right. Before he plays it, he always tunes it. To do this, he has to turn the keys. Turning the keys one way makes the strings get tighter. The sound goes higher. Turning the keys the other way makes the sound go lower. The strings get looser. Max can make his guitar sound right by changing the way the strings sound.

What is the main idea?

Max likes to make his guitar
_____
_____
sound right.
_____

Draw a line under some ways Max makes his guitar sound good.

Harcourt

Name _____

Writing Practice

Write to Describe

A. Make up a musical instrument. Draw a picture of your instrument. Give your instrument a name.

[drawing box]

My musical instrument is called a
_____
_____.

B. Write about your musical instrument. Describe how it sounds. Describe its pitch.

_____
_____
_____
_____
_____
_____

Harcourt

Name _____

Unit F, Chapter 1 Pushes and Pulls
What Makes Things Move?

LESSON 1
What Makes Things Move?

1. A _force_ is a push or a pull.

2. When you _push_ something, you press it away.

LESSON 2 What Are Some Ways Things Move?

1. Things move in many _different_ ways.

2. One way to tell how a thing moves is by the _path_ it makes.

LESSON 3 Why Do Things Move the Way They Do?

1. Motion changes when you _push_ or _pull_ something.

2. A hard push will move something _quickly_.

LESSON 4
How Do Objects Move on Surfaces?

1. Friction makes it _harder_ to move objects.

2. A _rough_ surface makes more friction than a smooth surface.

LESSON 5
How Do Wheels Help Objects Move?

1. A _wheel_ is a roller that turns on an axle.

2. Wheels and rollers make things _easier_ to push and pull.

Name _____

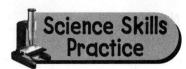

Investigate

These logs need to be moved from the pile
to the campfire.

1. Circle the things that could help you move
the logs.

2. Tell how you could move a pencil
across a desk.

_____

Answers will vary but should include

_____

pushing it with a hand.

_____

Harcourt

Name _____

What Makes Things Move?

Tell how each thing is being moved.
Write **push** or **pull**.

1. pull **2.** pull **3.** push

4. Show what the ball will do when the girl kicks it. Draw an arrow. Arrow should indicate the ball being kicked to a defensive player.

Harcourt

Name _____

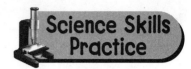
Group

1. Circle the toys you push. Make an **X** on the toys you pull.

2. Mark an **X** on objects that move easily with a gentle push.

Harcourt

Concept Review

What Are Some Ways Things Move?

Match the objects to the words that tell how each moves.

1. straight •

2. fast •

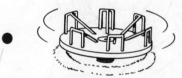

3. slow •

4. zigzag •

5. round and round •

6. back and forth •

Harcourt

Use with page F11.

Workbook • WB137

Name _____

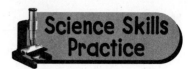

Predict

Kathy made a ramp. She put a marble at the top of her ramp.

1. What will happen when Kathy lets go of the marble? Draw a line to show where it will go.

Children should draw a line straight down the ramp.

2. This ramp is curved. Draw a line to show where Kathy's marble will go.

Children should draw a line that follows the curve of the ramp.

Harcourt

Use with page F12.

Why Do Things Move the Way They Do?

1. Circle the push that will make a toy car go a short way.

hard push

gentle push

2. Show how the soccer ball might change direction on the playing field. Draw arrows.

Arrows will vary but should indicate changing directions.

3. What will happen when the balls bump together? Write or draw your ideas.

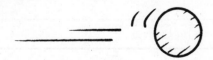 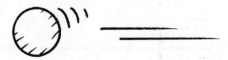

They will bounce back.

_____

Harcourt

Name _____

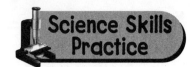

Measure

Marble 1

Marble 2

1. Measure how far each marble rolled. Write your answers.

_____   _____
6 centimeters   2 centimeters
_____   _____
Marble 1   Marble 2

2. Circle the marble that rolled the farthest. Tell why.

_____

Children should indicate that the marble on
a smooth surface will roll farther than one
on a rough surface.
_____

Harcourt

Name _____

How Do Surfaces Change the Way Objects Move?

Tell if each surface is **rough** or **smooth**.
Circle your answer.

1.

rough smooth

2.

rough (smooth)

3.

rough (smooth)

4.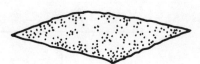

(rough) smooth

5. Circle the road with more friction.

Harcourt

Name _____

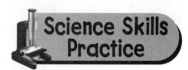

Science Skills
Practice

Draw a Conclusion

Mike and Jenny rode on different paths.

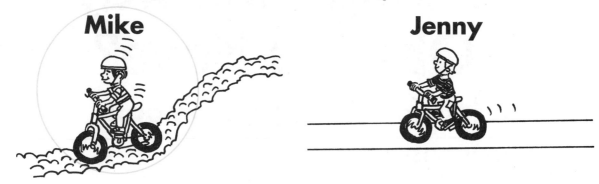

Mike   **Jenny**

1. Circle the child that would be more tired after the ride. Tell why.

_____

Mike was riding on a rough surface, which

_____

made it harder to pedal.

_____

2. Joyce made this toy. Draw something that you could add to make it easier to move.

Children should add wheels to the boxes.

Harcourt

Name _____

How Do Wheels Make Objects Easier to Move?

1. Draw wheels on the things that need wheels to move. Children should add wheels to the cart and bus.

2. Circle the thing that will make the refrigerator move the easiest.

 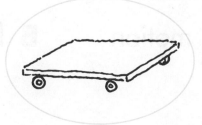

Harcourt

Name _____

Pushes and Pulls

Circle the word that best finishes each sentence.

1. When you ⎯⎯ something, you tug it closer
to you.

    A wheel   **B** push   **C** pull

2. A ⎯⎯ is a push or a pull.

    A surface   **B** force   **C** zigzag

3. When you ⎯⎯ something, you press it away
from you.

    A push   **B** pull   **C** motion

4. When two surfaces rub together, it is
called ⎯⎯.

    A motion   **B** zigzag   **C** friction

5. Moving from one place to another is
called ⎯⎯.

    A motion   **B** friction   **C** surface

Harcourt

Name _____

Identify Cause and Effect

Why Things Move the Way They Do

Susan and her classmates were playing volleyball. When the ball came to Susan, she hit it over the net. The other team members hit it back over. One time, the ball hit the pole on the net and bounced out of bounds. Another time, someone hit the ball very hard. The ball bounced high off the ground. Finish the chart.

Cause	Effect
The ball came to Susan.	She hit the ball over the net.
The ball hit the pole on the net.	The ball bounced out of bounds.
Someone hit the ball very hard.	The ball bounced high off the ground.

Harcourt

Use with page F16.

Workbook • WB145

Name _____

Write to Explain

A. Draw a picture of your favorite sport or game.

B. Draw circles around the pushes in the picture. Draw squares around the pulls in the picture.

C. Write about how your favorite sport or game uses pushes and pulls.

_____

- -

_____

- -

_____

- -

_____

Harcourt

Unit F, Chapter 2 Magnets

LESSON 1

What Are Magnets?

1. Magnets are pieces of _iron_ that attract things.

2. Magnets can only _attract_ things made of iron.

3. People use different kinds of _magnets_ in different ways.

LESSON 2

What Are the Poles of a Magnet?

1. Poles are places on a magnet where the pull is the _strongest_.

2. Every magnet has a _north_ pole and a _south_ pole.

3. Two poles that are the same _repel_ each other.

LESSON 3

What Can a Magnet Pull Through?

1. The pull of a magnet is called _magnetic_ force.

2. Magnetic force can pass through _paper_, water, air, _glass_, and _material_.

LESSON 4

How Can You Make a Magnet?

1. A magnet can _magnetize_ an object made of iron.

2. You can make a magnet by _stroking_ an iron object with a _magnet_.

Name _____

Record Data

Gather and circle the things that are pulled by a magnet. Make an **X** on the things that are **not** pulled by a magnet.

1.

paper clips

2.

wax paper

3.

steel nail

4.

candle

5.

scissors

6.

yarn

7. Record your data in this chart.

My Chart	
Pulled by a magnet	**NOT pulled by a magnet**
scissors nail paper clips	yarn candle wax paper

Harcourt

Use with page F32.

What Are Magnets?

Circle each object that a magnet would attract.

1.
leaf

2.
nail

3.
pencil

4.
thread

5.
key

6.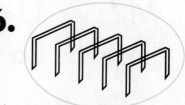
staples

Match each magnet to the words that tell what the magnet does.

7. picks things up •
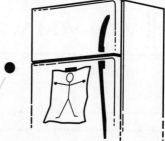

•

•

8. holds things together •
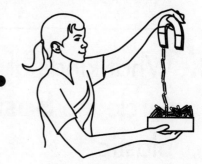

•

Name _____

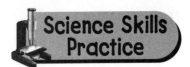

Infer

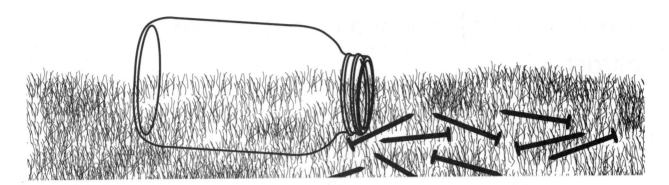

1. A man dropped a jar of nails in tall grass. What would you use to help him pick up the nails? Color the **best** answer. magnet

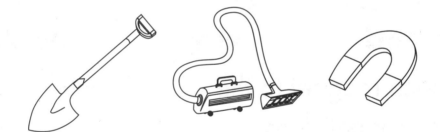

2. Tell why you would choose that item.

The nails are made from iron and are

attracted by the magnet.

3. What kinds of things would a magnet pick up? Circle the **best** answer.

plastic   wood   (iron)

Harcourt

Use with page F38.

Name _____

What Are the Poles of a Magnet?

1. Match each word to the picture it tells about.

repel •

attract •

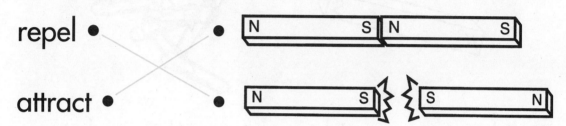

2. Write **S** and **N** to show how these magnets attract.

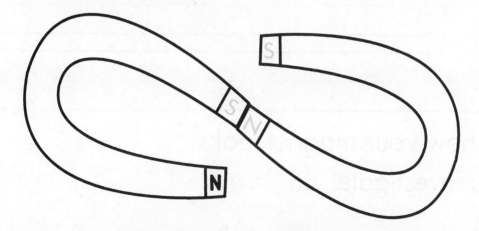

3. The magnet attracts iron bits. Color the parts of the magnet that have the strongest force.

The poles should be colored.

Harcourt

Name _____

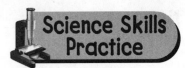

Plan an Investigation

How many paper clips can a magnet pick up?

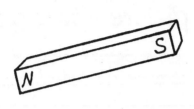

1. Tell how you could investigate this question.

Accept reasonable answers. Children may suggest
sticking the end of the magnet in the pile. Or they may

suggest holding the magnet and adding paper clips to
it one-by-one.

_____

_____

2. Draw how your magnet looks
as you investigate. Children should draw the
magnet with several paper clips
on it.

Harcourt

Name _____

What Can a Magnet Pull Through?

1. Joey wants to move a nail with a magnet. Circle the picture that will work the **best** for Joey.

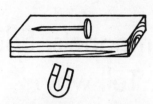  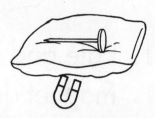

2. Circle all the things that the magnetic force of a small magnet can pass through.

  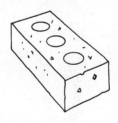 

3. Circle the things that can be attracted with magnetic force.

Harcourt

Name _____

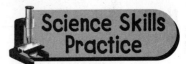

Draw a Conclusion

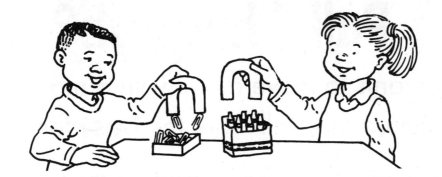

1. Edie and Harry are fishing with magnets. Edie's magnet does not lift the crayons. Tell why.

_____

Crayons are not made of iron.

_____

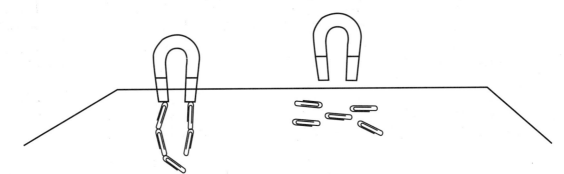

Magnet A   Magnet B

2. Magnet A lifted paper clips. Magnet B did not. Tell why.

_____

Magnet B is farther away from the paper

_____

clips than Magnet A.

_____

WB154 • Workbook   **Use with page F46.**

Harcourt

Name _____

How Can You Make a Magnet?

1. Color the objects that are magnetized.

Nail and scissors should be colored.

 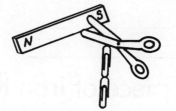 

2. Circle the object you would use to magnetize a nail.

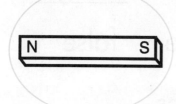  

3. How many paper clips have been magnetized?

one   two   five

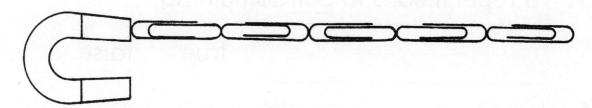

Harcourt

Name _____

Magnets

Circle **true** or **false**. If the sentence is false, write a word that would make it true.

1. <u>Attract</u> means to pull something.

_____

_____   (true)   false

2. A <u>pole</u> is a piece of iron that attracts things.

_____

magnet   true   (false)

3. How strongly a magnet pulls is its <u>strength</u>.

_____

_____   (true)   false

4. A magnet is <u>weakest</u> at its poles.

_____

strongest   true   (false)

5. To repel means to <u>pull</u> something.

_____

push   true   (false)

6. A magnet can <u>magnetize</u> a paper clip.

_____

_____   (true)   false

Harcourt

Name _____

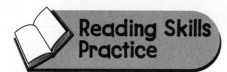

Draw Conclusions

Magnets Magnets attract things made of iron.
A magnet can magnetize, or give magnetic force
to, the things it attracts. Mr. Smith ran a key over
a magnet ten times the same
way. Then he used the key
to pick up some staples and
paper clips.

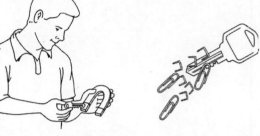

1. What did Mr. Smith do to his key?

He used his magnet to magnetize the key.

_____

_____

2. Why did Mr. Smith's key pick up staples and
paper clips?

Because the staples and paper clips have iron

_____

_____

that attracts them to the magnet.

Harcourt

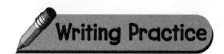

Write Directions

A. Make up a game or a toy that uses magnets. Draw your game or toy in the box.

B. Write directions for playing your game or using your toy. Tell what to do first, next, and last.

First _____

Next _____

Last _____

Harcourt

Unit Experiments
Grade 1

Harcourt

1. Observe and ask a question.

_____

_____

_____

_____

_____

_____

_____

2. Form a hypothesis.

A hypothesis is a suggested answer to the question you are investigating. You must be able to do a fair test of the hypothesis.

_____

_____

_____

_____

_____

3. Plan a fair test.

What things will you keep the same in the test? Write or draw them here.

Harcourt

4. What is one thing you will change in the test?

_____
- -
_____
_____
- -
_____

5. What objects will you need to do the test? List or draw them here.

6. What steps will you take to do the test? List or draw them here.

Harcourt

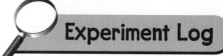
7. Do the test.

Record your data in a chart.

8. Draw conclusions.
Communicate results.

What are your results? How can you communicate your results to others?

_____

_____

_____

_____

_____

_____

Harcourt

Seeds and Water

Observe and ask a question.

1. What question can you ask about what seeds need to sprout?

Do seeds need water to sprout?

Form a hypothesis.

2. What is something you think is true about what seeds need to sprout?

Seeds need water to sprout.

Plan a fair test.

3. What things will you keep the same in your test? Write or draw them here.

I will put cotton and a paper towel in each plastic cup. I will put both cups in the same place. I will use the same number of seeds in each cup. I will use the same type of seeds in each cup.

Harcourt

4. What one thing will you change in your test?

I will add water to the cotton and paper towel in one of the cups.

5. What things will you need to do your test? Write or draw them here.

I will use two plastic cups, cotton, paper towels, radish seeds, and water.

6. What steps will you take to do your test?

a. Tie the string through the holes my teacher makes in the plates.

b. Use a marker to label one cup WET and one cup DRY.

c. Fill the center of each cup with cotton.

d. Place ten seeds between the paper towel and the sides of each cup.

e. Add water to moisten the cotton and paper towel in one cup.

f. Each day, check to see if any seeds have sprouted.

g. Add water as needed to keep the seeds moist in one cup.

Harcourt

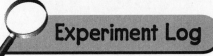
● Do the test.

7. Record your data in the chart.

Did Seeds Sprout Roots?

	Moist Seeds	Dry Seeds
Day 1		
Day 2		
Day 3		
Day 4		
Day 5		
Day 6		
Day 7		

Draw conclusions. Communicate results.

8. What are your results? How can you communicate your results to others?

_____

_____

_____

_____

_____

_____

Harcourt

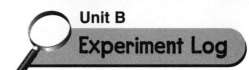
Animal Coverings

Observe and ask a question.

1. What can you ask about how body coverings help animals?

Do body coverings keep animals warm? Do body coverings help hide animals?

Form a hypothesis.

2. What is something you think is true about how body coverings help animals?

Body coverings keep animals warm.

Plan a fair test.

3. What things will you keep the same in the test? Write or draw them here.

I will compare body coverings in the same environment. I will make my observations the same way.

Harcourt

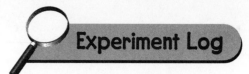

4. What one thing will you change in the test?

I will change the kind of body covering observed.

5. What objects will you need to do the test? Write or draw them here.

ice cubes, cold water, large container, wool sock, plastic bag, newspaper

6. What steps will you take to do the test?

a. Put ice cubes and cold water in the container.

b. Put the bag on one hand and place the hand in the container. Observe.

c. Wrap newspaper around the hand. Put the bag over the newspaper. Place the hand in the container. Observe.

d. Put the hand in the sock. Put the bag over the sock. Place the hand in the container. Observe.

Harcourt

Name _____

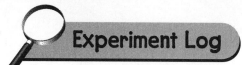

Do the test.

7. Record your data in the chart.

How Did the Covered Hand Feel?

Body Covering	Observation

Draw conclusions. Communicate results.

8. What are your results? How can you communicate your results to others?

_____

_____

_____

_____

Harcourt

Name _____

Clean Air

Observe and ask a question.

1. Air is dirty in some places. It is clean in other places. Ask a question about air in different places.

Where is air the cleanest?

_____

Form a hypothesis.

2. Where do you think air is the cleanest?

Air is cleanest indoors.

_____

Plan a fair test.

3. What things will you keep the same in the test? Write or draw them here.

I will use the same amount of petroleum jelly on each plate. I will smear it in a circle that is the same size on each plate. I will use the same size plate. I will leave all the plates in their places for the same amount of time.

Harcourt

4. What one thing will you change in the test?

I will put each plate in a different place.

5. What things will you need to do the test? Write or draw them here.

I will use small foam plates, petroleum jelly, a large plastic measuring spoon, string or yarn, a permanent marker, and a magnifying glass.

6. What steps will you take to do the test?

a. Tie the string through the holes my teacher makes in the plates.

b. Number the plates and write down where each plate will go.

c. Smear one spoonful of petroleum jelly onto each plate.

d. Find places to put the plates where they won't be disturbed. Put some plates indoors and some plates outdoors. Use the string to tie down the plates that are placed outdoors.

e. Leave the plates in their places for the same amount of time.

f. Collect the plates.

g. Use the magnifying glass to see what has collected on the plates.

Harcourt

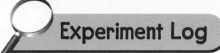
Do the test.

7. Record your data in the chart.

Where Is Air the Dirtiest?

Plate Number	Where It Was	Things I See

Draw conclusions. Communicate results.

8. What are your results? How can you communicate your results to others?

_____

_____

_____

_____

_____

Harcourt

Heat and Water

Observe and ask a question.

1. The sun gives off heat. Can the sun's heat change water? Ask a question about the way heat can change water.

Does heat make water get warmer?

Form a hypothesis.

2. How do you think heat changes water?

Heat will make water get warmer.

Plan a fair test.

3. What things will you keep the same in your test? Write or draw them here.

I will use cups that are the same color and size. I will put the same amount of water in each cup. I will use the same kind of thermometer. I will record the temperatures at the same time of day.

Harcourt

4. What is one thing you will change in your test?

I will change the location of each cup.

5. What things will you need for your test?
Write or draw them here.

I will use two large foam cups that are the
same size and color, a measuring cup, water,
two thermometers that are the same, and a
dark place and a sunny place.

6. What steps will you take to do your test?

a. Measure a certain amount of water and pour
it into one of the foam cups.

b. Measure the same amount of water and pour it
into the other cup.

c. Put a thermometer into each cup and record
the original temperature.

d. Put one cup in a sunny place.

e. Put the other cup in a dark place.

f. Record the temperatures at the same time at
least two times during the day.

g. Record the temperatures at the same three
times every day for one week.

Harcourt

Name _____

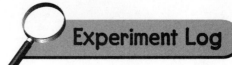

Do the test.

7. Record your data in the chart.

How Does the Sun's Heat Change Water?

Morning Temperature	Noon Temperature	Afternoon Temperature

Draw conclusions. Communicate results.

8. What are your results? How can you communicate your results to others?

_____

- -

_____

- -

_____

- -

_____

Harcourt

Solids in Water

Observe and ask a question.

1. What can you ask about the way that solids dissolve in water of different temperatures?

How does water temperature change the way
solids dissolve? Which solids dissolve more easily
in warm water than in cold water?

Form a hypothesis.

2. What could be true about how water temperature changes the way salt and sugar dissolve?

Water temperature does not change the way salt
and sugar dissolve in water.

Plan a fair test.

3. What things will you keep the same in the test? Write or draw them here.

I will use the same amount of water and solid
each time. Both the hot and cold water should be

Harcourt

about the same temperature each time. I will stir
at about the same speed each time.

4. What is one thing you will change in the test?

I will change only the water temperature.

5. What objects will you need to do the test?
Write or draw them here.

plastic cups, spoons, measuring cups, marker, hot
water, cold water, sugar, salt, timer, thermometer

6. What steps will you take to do the test?

a. Label 4 containers: "COLD SALT," "HOT SALT,"
   "COLD SUGAR," "HOT SUGAR."

b. Measure hot tap water into two of the
   containers.

c. Measure cold tap water into the other two
   containers.

d. Stir a spoonful of sugar into the "HOT SUGAR"
   container. Time how long it takes the crystals
   to dissolve completely. Write what happens.

e. Do the same thing for "HOT SALT."

f. Do the steps again with the sugar and salt for
   the cold containers.

Harcourt

Name _____

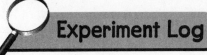

● Do the test.

7. Record your data in the chart.

How Does Water Temperature Change the Way Solids Dissolve?

Name of Solid	Cold Water	Hot Water
	Dissolving time: _____ seconds	Dissolving time: _____ seconds
	Dissolving time: _____ seconds	Dissolving time: _____ seconds

Draw conclusions. Communicate results.

8. What are your results? How can you communicate your results to others?

_____

_____

_____

_____

_____

Harcourt

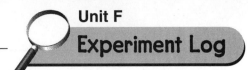
Height and Distance

Observe and ask a question.

1. What can you ask about the way height affects distance?

How does the height of a ramp change how
far a toy truck will go?

Form a hypothesis.

2. What could be true about the way a change in height changes the distance a toy truck will go?

Making one end of a ramp higher will make a toy
truck go farther.

Plan a fair test.

3. What things will you keep the same in the test? Write or draw them here.

I will use the same toy truck, the same board, and
the same rolling surface each time. I will start the
truck at the same place each time.

Harcourt

4. What is one thing you will change in the test?

I will change the height of the ramp.

5. What objects will you need to do the test? Write or draw them here.

I will use a toy truck, board, books, meterstick, roll of paper, and pencil.

6. What steps will you take to do the test?

a. Put one end of a board on one or two books. Measure the height of the ramp.

b. Put a toy truck at the top. Let it roll down the ramp.

c. Use the roll of paper to measure how far the toy truck rolled after leaving the ramp.

d. Repeat these steps three times. Raise the ramp each time by adding more books.

Harcourt

Do the test.

7. Record your data in the chart.

How Does the Height of a Ramp Change How Far a Toy Truck Will Go?

Height of Ramp (Board)	Distance the Truck Rolls

Draw conclusions. Communicate results.

8. What are your results? How can you communicate your results to others?

_____
_____
_____
_____
_____
_____

Harcourt

DATE DUE

Demco